INGENIOUS

LATERAL THINKING PUZZLES

Paul Sloane & Des MacHale

Illustrated by Myron Miller

Sterling Publishing Co., Inc.
New York

Edited by Peter Gordon

Library of Congress Cataloging-in-Publication Data Available

10 9 8 7 6 5 4 3 2

Published by Sterling Publishing Company, Inc.
387 Park Avenue South, New York, N.Y. 10016
© 1998 by Paul Sloane and Des MacHale
Distributed in Canada by Sterling Publishing
c/o Canadian Manda Group, One Atlantic Avenue, Suite 105
Toronto, Ontario, Canada M6K 3E7
Distributed in Great Britain and Europe by Cassell PLC
Wellington House, 125 Strand, London WC2R 0BB, England
Distributed in Australia by Capricorn Link (Australia) Pty Ltd.
P.O. Box 6651, Baulkham Hills, Business Centre, NSW 2153, Australia

Sterling ISBN 0-8069-4779-9

Acknowledgments

Many people contributed ideas for this book. Some come from the lateral thinking forum on the Internet at www.books.com. We would particularly like to acknowledge and thank the following people for their contributions: Jean-Claude Franc for "Hosing Down"; Darren Rigby for "One Mile," "You Can't Be Too Careful," and "Don't Get Up"; Peter Bloxsom for "Garbage Nosiness," "Fired for Joining Mensa," and "Dali's Brother"; Wei-Hwa Huang for "Flipping Pages"; Robert Burnett for "The Power of Tourism"; John D. van Pelt for "Pass Protection" and "Leadfoot and Gumshoe"; Michael Boguslavsky for "The Man Who Got Water."

Jackie, Hannah, Ann, and Val Sloane helped edit the book and write the clues.

CONTENTS

Instructions 7

The Puzzles 9

Warm-Up Puzzles 10

Workout Puzzles 18

Strenuous Puzzles 26

Super-Strenuous Puzzles 39

The Clues 49

The Answers 73

About the Authors 93

Index 94

INSTRUCTIONS

1. Grab some other people. It's better to do these puzzles in a group of two or more than to try to solve them individually. Typically, they contain insufficient information for you to deduce the solution. You need to ask questions in order to gather more information before you can formulate solutions.
2. Start with the "Warm-Up Puzzles." They are a little easier.
3. One person acts as quizmaster. He or she reads the puzzle out loud and reads the solution silently.
4. The people trying to solve the puzzle ask questions in order to gather information, check assumptions, and test possible solutions.
5. The quizmaster can answer in one of four ways: "Yes," "No," "Irrelevant," or "Please rephrase the question."
6. If the solvers get stuck, the quizmaster can offer one or more of the clues given in the "Clues" section.
7. The aim is to arrive at the solution given in the "Answers" section, not simply to find a situation that satisfies the initial conditions. If you want to award points for good alternatives, you can, but the answer given is the true goal.
8. The person who solves the puzzle gets the kudos, recognition, and prestige. Credit should also be given to those who ask the key lateral questions.
9. Strategy tip: Test your assumptions, and ask broad questions that establish general conditions, motives, and actions. Don't narrow in on specific solutions until you have first established the broad parameters of what's going on.
10. When you get stuck, attack the problem from a new direction—think laterally! Have fun!

THE PUZZLES

Warm-Up Puzzles

Angry Response

A man called his wife from the office to say that he would be home at around eight o'clock. He got in at two minutes past eight. His wife was extremely angry at his late arrival. Why?

Clues: 51/Answer: 74.

Picture Purchase

An art expert went to a sale and bought a picture he knew to be worthless. Why?

Clues: 63/Answer: 84.

Alone in a Boat

Why are two little animals alone in a little boat in the middle of the ocean?

Clues: 50/Answer: 74.

Strangulation

A famous dancer was found strangled. The police did not suspect murder. Why not?

Clues: 67/Answer: 87.

Complete Garbage

∙∙

The garbage was emptied out of the cans and a man died. How?

Clues: 54/Answer: 77.

Golf Bag

∙∙

During a golf competition, Paul's ball ended up in a bunker inside a little brown paper bag that had blown onto the course. He was told that he must either play the ball in the bag or take the ball out of the bag and incur a one stroke penalty. What did he do?

Clues: 58/Answer: 80.

Flipping Pages

Yesterday, I went through a book, which I had already read, in a peculiar manner. After I finished a page, I flipped to the next page, then rotated the book 180 degrees. After that page, I rotated the book 180 degrees and then flipped to the next page, rotated the book 180 degrees again, and continued in this fashion until I was done with the whole book. What was going on?

Clues: 56/Answer: 79.

Leadfoot and Gumshoe

A woman is stopped for speeding. The police officer gives her a warning, but the woman insists that she be given a ticket and a fine, which she promptly pays. Why did she want the ticket and fine?

Clues: 59/Answer: 81.

Man in Tights

A man wearing tights is lying unconscious in a field. Next to him is a rock. What happened?

Clues: 59/Answer: 81.

Straight Ahead

When the Eisenhower Interstate Highway System was built, it was specified that one mile in every five must be absolutely straight. Why?

Clues: 67/Answer: 87.

Motion Not Passed

A referendum motion was not passed. If more people had voted against it, however, it would have passed. How come?

Clues: 60/Answer: 82.

Russian Racer

At the height of the Cold War, a U.S. racing car easily beat a Russian car in a two-car race. How did the Russian newspapers truthfully report this in order to make it look as though the Russian car had outdone the American car?

Clues: 65/Answer: 85.

Waterless Rivers

Now for a riddle: What has rivers but no water, cities but no buildings, and forests but no trees?

Clues: 70/Answer: 89.

The Test

The teacher gave Ben and Jerry a written test. Ben read the test, then folded his arms and answered none of the questions. Jerry carefully wrote out good answers to the questions. When the time was up, Ben handed in a blank sheet of paper while Jerry handed in his work. The teacher gave Ben an A and Jerry a C. Why?

Clues: 68/Answer: 87.

Statue of an Insect

•••

Why is there a commemorative statue of an insect in a little town in the state of Alabama?

Clues: 67/Answer: 87.

Fired for Joining Mensa

•••

Mensa is a club for clever people. Anne's employer has no anti-Mensa feeling, but has made it clear to her that if she ever joins Mensa she will lose her job. How come?

Clues: 56/Answer: 79.

Six-Foot Drop

A man standing on solid concrete dropped a tomato six feet, but it did not break or bruise. How come?

Clues: 66/Answer: 86.

Seven Bells

A little shop in New York is called The Seven Bells, yet it has eight bells hanging outside. Why?

Clues: 65–66/Answer: 85.

Reentry

What took 19 years to get into itself?

Clues: 64/Answer: 84.

Assault and Battery

John is guilty of no crime, but he is surrounded by professional people, one of whom hits him until he cries. Why?

Clues: 51/Answer: 74.

Up in the Air

One hundred feet up in the air, it lies with its back on the ground. What is it?

Clues: 69/Answer: 88.

Clean-Shaven

Why did Alexander the Great order all his men to shave?

Clues: 54/Answer: 77.

Adolf Hitler

During the war, a British soldier had Adolf Hitler clearly in the sights of his gun. Why didn't he fire?

Clues: 50/Answer: 74.

Winning Numbers

I have on a piece of paper the winning numbers in next week's lotto jackpot. I am an avid gambler, yet I feel I have very little chance of winning. Why?

Clues: 70/Answer: 89.

Fair Fight

A boxer left the ring after winning the world championship. His trainer took all the money and he never got a cent. Why not?

Clues: 56/Answer: 78.

Unknown Recognition

I saw a man I had never seen before, but I immediately knew who he was. He was not famous and had never been described to me. He was not unusual nor doing anything unusual. How did I recognize him?

Clues: 69/Answer: 88.

Riddle of the Sphinx

The Sphinx asked this famous riddle: What is it that goes on four legs in the morning, two legs in the afternoon, and three legs in the evening?

Clues: 64/Answer: 85.

Unclimbed

Why has no one climbed the largest known extinct volcano?

Clues: 69/Answer: 88.

Talking to Herself

A woman is talking sadly. Nobody can understand her, but a man is filming her intently. Why?

Clues: 68/Answer: 87.

Workout Puzzles

The Unlucky Bed

A certain bed in a certain hospital acquires the reputation of being unlucky. Whatever patient is assigned to this bed seems to die there on a Friday evening. A watch is kept by camera and the reason is discovered. What is it?

Clues: 69/Answer: 88.

Missing Items

What two items does a boy have at 10 years of age that he did not have when he was 1 year old?

Clues: 59/Answer: 82.

Once Too Often

If you do it once, it's good. If you do it twice on the same day, though, it's a serious crime. What is it?

Clues: 61/Answer: 83.

Noteworthy

A woman took a picture of a U.S. president to her bank. As a result a criminal was arrested. How?

Clues: 61/Answer: 83.

Rejected Shoes

A man bought a pair of shoes that were in good condition and that fit him well. He liked the style and they looked good. However, after he had worn them for one day he took them back to the shop and asked for a refund. Why?

Clues: 64/Answer: 84.

Slow Drive

Why does a man drive his car on a long journey at a steady 15 miles per hour? The speed limit is well above that and his car is in full working order and capable of high speeds.

Clues: 67/Answer: 86.

Weak Case

The police charged a man with a crime. They had a weak case against him. He posted his bail. The police then had a strong case against him. Why?

Clues: 70/Answer: 89.

The Man Who Got Water

A man parked his car on the road, walked into a building, returned with some water, and poured the water onto the sidewalk. Why?

Clues: 59/Answer: 81.

The Writer

A man who was paralyzed in his arms, legs, and mouth, and unable to speak a word, wrote a best-selling book. How?

Clues: 71/Answer: 90.

Chimney Problem

An industrial archaeologist was examining an abandoned factory in a remote place with no one in sight or within earshot. He climbed to the top of an old 100-foot chimney by means of a rusty old ladder attached to the outside of the chimney. When he got to the top, the ladder fell away, leaving him stranded. How did he get down?

Clues: 54/Answer: 77.

Happy Birthday

A man went into his local shopping center. A woman whom he had never met before wished him a happy birthday. How did she know it was his birthday?

Clues: 58/Answer: 80.

Acidic Action

A murderer killed his wife and dissolved her body completely in a bath of acid. What piece of evidence caused him to be caught?

Clues: 50/Answer: 74.

November 11

A large mail order company performed an analysis of its customers. It was surprised to learn that an unusually large number were born on November 11. How could this be?

Clues: 61/Answer: 83.

Garbage Nosiness

One morning last week I peered into my neighbor's garbage can and then drove to work feeling annoyed. One morning this week I peered into my other neighbor's garbage can and then drove off feeling even more annoyed. Why?

Clues: 57/Answer: 79.

Well-Meaning

How did an animal rights activist who had good intentions cause the death of the living creatures she was trying to save?

Clues: 70/Answer: 89.

Shooting a Dead Man

A policeman shot a dead man. He was not acting illegally. Why did he do it?

Clues: 66/Answer: 86.

Bottled Up

A cleaning woman asked the man she worked for if she could take home his empty bottles. When she got home, she threw them out. Why did she do this?

Clues: 53/Answer: 75.

Alex Ferguson

In the early 1990s, Alex Ferguson was the coach of Manchester United, the most successful professional soccer team in England at that time. Previously he had been a very successful manager in Scotland. He would be a very successful manager of a soccer team anywhere in the world, except Singapore. Why is that?

Clues: 50/Answer: 74.

Don't Get Up

A woman is reading a newspaper alone. She hears the phone ring in the room next to the one she is in. Although she knows that the call is probably important, she does not bother to answer it. Why not?

Clues: 55/Answer: 77.

Misunderstood

Part of the police manual gives instructions in a language that none of the policemen speaks. Why?

Clues: 60/Answer: 82.

Scuba Do

Why was a man driving down the street wearing a scuba face mask?

Clues: 65/Answer: 85.

WALLY Test I

From the World Association of Learning, Laughter, and Youth (WALLY) comes the WALLY Test! It is a set of quick-fire questions. They may look easy, but be warned—they are designed to trick you. Write down your answers on a piece of paper and then see how many you got right. The time limit is three minutes.

1. What is the last thing you take off before going to bed at night?
2. What gets longer when it is cut at both ends?
3. What was the first name of King George VI of England?
4. What do you call a fly without wings?
5. How many squares are there on a standard chessboard?
6. How many seconds are there in a year?
7. A man throws a ball three feet, it stops, and then returns to his hand without touching anything. How come?
8. What was the largest island in the world before Australia was discovered?
9. Why can a policeman never open the door in his pajamas?
10. If 5 dogs kill 5 rats in 5 minutes, how long does it take 15 dogs to kill 15 rats?

Answers on page 91.

Strenuous Puzzles

One Mile

If you go to your atlas and look at the western edge of the state of South Dakota where it borders Montana, you will see a straight line with a kink of about one mile. Everywhere else the border is a straight line. The kink does not benefit any local landowner and no other states are involved. Why is the kink there?

Clues: 61–62/Answer: 83.

The Unbroken Arm
....

Why did a perfectly healthy young girl put a full plaster cast on her arm when it was not injured in any way?

Clues: 68/Answer: 88.

The Shoplifter
....

A shoplifter starts stealing small items and over a period of time steals larger and larger items, but then suddenly stops altogether. What is going on?

Clues: 66/Answer: 86.

Getting Away with Murder

A man shot his wife dead. She was not threatening him or anyone else. He then gave himself up to the police. They released him. Why?

Clues: 57/Answer: 80.

Exceptional Gratitude

Why did Bill thank Ted for some eggs that Bill had never received and that Ted had never given?

Clues: 55/Answer: 78.

Dali's Brother

Some time after Salvador Dali's death, his younger brother became famous as (believe it or not) a surrealist painter. This younger brother had great international success and the word "genius" was used to describe him. His name was Dali and he did not change it. Yet today, the world remembers only one Dali and few people even know that he had a brother. Why is this?

Clues: 54/Answer: 77.

Bare Bones

During an examination, a medical student is handed a human femur (thigh bone). The examiner asks the student, "How many of these do you have?"

The student replies, "Five."

"Wrong," says the examiner, "You have two femurs."

But the student was right. How come?

Clues: 52/Answer: 75.

Two Clocks

A man was given two clocks by his wife as a Christmas present. He did not collect clocks and they already had plenty of clocks in the house. However, he was very pleased to receive them. Why?

Clues: 68/Answer: 88.

The Power of Tourism

In a certain place the local authorities, in order to increase tourism, have made the price of electricity higher. Why?

Clues: 63/Answer: 84.

Wiped Out

A woman got a job with a large company. After her first day's work she returned home utterly exhausted because of a misunderstanding. What had happened?

Clues: 71/Answer: 89.

88 Too Big

A man died because his number was 88 too big. How come?

Clues: 55/Answer: 78.

Invisible

What can you stand in front of in broad daylight and not see, even if you have perfect eyesight?

Clues: 58/Answer: 81.

The Auction

••

A man went to an auction to bid for something he wanted. He expected to pay about $100 for it, but ended up paying $500. There was no minimum price and no one bid against him. What happened?

Clues: 52/Answer: 75.

Poor Investment

••

Why did a company spend millions of dollars trying to find something that costs only a few thousand dollars?

Clues: 63/Answer: 84.

Nonexistent Actors

Why did the credits of a well-known movie list the names of four nonexistent actors?

Clues: 60/Answer: 82.

Machine Forge

A man builds a machine into which he feeds colored paper. Out of the other side come perfect $100 bills. Experts cannot tell them from real ones. How does he do it and why does he sell the machine?

Clues: 59/Answer: 81.

Spraying the Grass

The groundskeeper at a sports complex watered the grass every evening when the sun was setting. The grass grew fine. Before a major event, though, he sprayed the grass during the midday heat. Why?

Clues: 67/Answer: 86.

Wonder Horse

A horse that had lost every one of its previous races was entered in a horse race and came in first ahead of a top-class field. No drugs were used, and if the jockey had not confessed, then nobody would have known. What happened?

Clues: 71/Answer: 90.

Adrift in the Ocean

Two men are in a boat drifting in the Atlantic Ocean a hundred miles from the nearest land. They have no drinking water onboard, no radio, and they have no contact with any other boats or people. Yet they survive for a long time. How?

Clues: 50/Answer: 74.

Promotion

John is a young man working for a big company. He is lazy, poorly motivated, and inefficient. Yet he is the first person in his department to be promoted. Why?

Clues: 63/Answer: 84.

Barren Patch

A farmer has a patch of ground in the middle of one of his most fertile fields on which nothing will grow. Why not?

Clues: 52/Answer: 75.

Job Description

Two men were sitting in a crowded restaurant. A woman who was a total stranger to both of them walked in and told them her job. She said nothing more and they said nothing. What was going on?

Clues: 58–59/Answer: 81.

No More Bore

A notorious bore once called on Winston Churchill, who sent his butler to the door to say that Churchill was not at home. What suggestion did Churchill make to the butler to convince the caller that he really was not at home?

Clues: 60/Answer: 82.

Shaking a Fist

A policeman stopped a man for dangerous driving. As the policeman walked toward the car, the man rolled down the window and waved his fist at the policeman. Later, he thanked the policeman for saving his life. Why?

Clues: 66/Answer: 86.

Burnt Wood

Over the past 100 years many men have dedicated significant portions of their lives to the quest for some burnt wood. Although they have sometimes been successful, the burnt wood has never moved. What is it?

Clues: 53/Answer: 75–76.

The Wrong Ball

A golfer drove his ball out of sight over a hill. When he got there, he saw a ball that was the same make as his own and identical to it in every way. But he knew immediately that it was not his ball. How come?

Clues: 71/Answer: 90.

Window Pain

A builder builds a house that has a square window. It is two feet high and two feet wide. It is not covered by anything. The person for whom the house is being built decides that the window does not give enough light. He tells the builder to change the window so that it gives twice the amount of light. It must be in the same wall, and it must be a square window that is two feet high and two feet wide. How does the builder accomplish this task?

Clues: 70/Answer: 89.

Gas Attack

A man was sentenced to ten years' imprisonment with hard labor because he had kept the gas mask that the army had issued him. Why?

Clues: 57/Answer: 80.

WALLY Test II

Time for another WALLY Test. The questions may look easy, but be warned—they're designed to trip you up. Write down your answers on a piece of paper and then see how many you got right. The time limit is three minutes.

1. Rearrange these letters to make one new word: NEW NEW DOOR
2. What do you find in seconds, minutes, and centuries, but not in days, years, or decades?
3. Which is correct: "Seven eights are 54" or "Seven eights is 54"?
4. Three men in a boat each had a cigarette, but they had no match, fire, or lighter. How did they light the cigarettes?
5. A clock strikes 6 in five seconds. How long does it take to strike 12?
6. What was the U.S. president's name in 1984?
7. Who won an Oscar for Best Actor and an Olympic gold medal for sprinting?
8. If two men can dig two holes in two days, how long does it take one man to dig half a hole?
9. An 80-year-old prisoner was kept inside a high security prison with all the doors locked. He broke out. How?
10. If the post office clerk refused to stick a $4 stamp on your package, would you stick it on yourself?

Answers on page 92.

Super-Strenuous Puzzles

Bald Facts

A woman fell in love and, as a result, lost all her hair. Why?

Clues: 52/Answer: 75.

Fingerprint Evidence

The mass murderer Ted Bundy was very careful never to leave any fingerprints at the scene of any of his crimes, and he never did. Yet fingerprint evidence helped to incriminate him. How come?

Clues: 56/Answer: 79.

Hosing Down

Because it was raining, the firemen hosed down the road. Why?

Clues: 58/Answer: 80–81.

Pentagon Puzzle

The headquarters of the U.S. defense operations is the Pentagon in Arlington, Virginia. Why does it have twice as many bathrooms as it needs?

Clues: 62–63/Answer: 83.

Fill Her Up!

A woman bought her husband a beautiful new sports car as a present. When he first saw it, he filled it with wet cement and completely ruined it. Why?

Clues: 56/Answer: 78–79.

Three Spirals

A woman was pleased when she received three spirals instead of the usual two. When it was discovered that she had received three spirals, she was arrested. Why?

Clues: 68/Answer: 87.

You Can't Be Too Careful

Millions of people buy a particular medicine. The disease for which the medicine is effective is one that these people have virtually no chance of catching. What do they buy?

Clues: 71/Answer: 90.

Nonconventional

In a convent, the novice nuns at the dinner table are not allowed to ask for anything such as the salt from the other end of the table. This is because they should be so aware of one another's needs that they should not need to ask. How do they get around this prohibition?

Clues: 60/Answer: 82.

Replacing the Leaves

During fall, a little girl was in her backyard trying to stick the fallen leaves back onto the trees with glue. Why?

Clues: 64/Answer: 85.

Secret Assignment

The famous physicist Ulam one day noticed that several of his best graduate students had disappeared from his university. They had in fact gone to Los Alamos to take part in the top-secret preparations for the first atomic bomb. They were sworn to secrecy. How did Ulam find out where they had gone?

Clues: 65/Answer: 85.

The Ransom Note

A kidnapper sent a ransom note. He prepared it carefully and ensured that it contained no fingerprints. Yet it was used to prove his guilt. How?

Clues: 64/Answer: 84.

Debugging

How were insects once used in the diagnosis of a serious disease?

Clues: 55/Answer: 77.

Biography

An author died because he wrote a biography. How did he die?

Clues: 52/Answer: 75.

Ancient Antics

We generally consider ourselves to be a lot smarter and better educated than the people who lived in the prehistoric periods of the Stone Age, Iron Age, and Bronze Age. But what was it that men and women did in those times that no man or woman has managed to achieve for the last 4000 years?

Clues: 51/Answer: 74.

Cartoon Character

What cartoon character owes his existence to a misprint in a scientific journal?

Clues: 54/Answer: 76.

The Carpet Seller

I bought a beautiful plain carpet measuring 9 feet by 16 feet from the carpet seller. When I got home I realized that my room was actually 12 feet by 12 feet. I returned to the carpet seller, who assured me that I could now exactly fit my room, provided I made just one cut to the original piece. Can you figure out how to do it?

Clues: 53/Answer: 76.

No Response

A man often answered questions in the course of his work. One day a stranger asked him a perfectly reasonable question that he refused to answer. Why?

Clues: 61/Answer: 82.

Walking Backward

A man walked backward from the front door of his house to his kitchen. Someone rang the doorbell and the man ran quickly out of his back door. Why?

Clues: 69/Answer: 88–89.

Free Lunch

A man in a restaurant used two forks and one knife. He did not pay for his lunch. What was happening?

Clues: 57/Answer: 79.

Right Off

A man comes out of his house to find that his new car is damaged beyond repair after he has paid for it but before he has had time to insure it. However, he is absolutely delighted at what has happened. Why?

Clues: 65/Answer: 85.

Business Rivalry

Cain and Abel are business rivals. Cain cuts his price, and Abel then undercuts him. Cain then cuts his price even lower than Abel. Abel slashes his price to a ridiculous level and gets all the business, forcing Cain out of the market. But Cain has the last laugh. Why?

Clues: 53/Answer: 76.

Full Refund

A young couple went to a theater to watch a movie. After 15 minutes they decided to leave. They had had a perfectly good view of the movie, which was running in perfect order. The cashier gave them a full refund. Why?

Clues: 57/Answer: 79.

A Day at the Races

A man was returning from a day at the races where he had made a lot of money. He was speeding in his car and was stopped by the police. The policeman took down all his details, but the man was never prosecuted or suffered any penalty. Why not?

Clues: 55/Answer: 77.

Pass Protection

In the city where I live, commuters on the mass transit system can use monthly passes or single tokens. Today, I saw long lines of commuters waiting to buy passes and tokens. Those people with passes or tokens were able to bypass the lines. However, even though I had neither a pass nor a token, I was also able to walk right up to the turnstiles and pass through. How come?

Clues: 62/Answer: 83.

THE CLUES

Acidic Action

He disposed of her clothes and jewelry.

Her body was completely dissolved in acid.

A trace of her was found and identified.

Adolf Hitler

It was the real Adolf Hitler, the one who led the German Third Reich.

Adolf Hitler was alive at the time, and the war still had much time to run.

The British soldier did not recognize Hitler. But it would have made no difference if he had.

Adrift in the Ocean

They found a source of drinking water.

No rain or ice is involved.

They were in a particular location.

Alex Ferguson

Soccer is played in Singapore.

Alex Ferguson's style of coaching would be appropriate.

One of his personal habits would not be acceptable in Singapore.

Alone in a Boat

They were deliberately cast adrift from a famous boat.

The animals can sometimes offend the senses.

Ancient Antics

It has to do with nourishment.

It does not involve a particular strength or physical skill.

It concerns animals.

Angry Response

She was angry because he was late.

They had no particular appointment at eight o'clock.

Assault and Battery

John is healthy.

The person who hits John does it to help him.

It is a common occurrence.

The Auction

He was bidding for a pet.

The creature had a talent.

He thought he was in a competitive auction.

Bald Facts

Her hair loss was part of a greater misfortune that befell her.

She did not lose her hair from natural causes.

Her choice of lover was important.

Bare Bones

The student was healthy and was not physically abnormal.

She had never had any kind of medical operation.

Every human is born with two femurs.

Barren Patch

The patch of land received the same sunlight and rain as the fertile land around it.

The patch is an irregular shape.

No one had ever gone there, but human action had made the land barren.

Biography

His death was accidental.

Had he chosen a different subject for a biography, he would not have died.

The author died a similar death to that suffered by the subject of his biography.

Bottled Up

The bottles remained unbroken, unchanged, and unused throughout.

They were worthless when empty, but had been expensive when full.

She was status-conscious.

Burnt Wood

The wood has a symbolic value, but is not in itself rare or valuable.

The men involved in this quest all speak English yet come from countries far apart.

They compete over many weeks.

Business Rivalry

Cain uses Abel's lower prices to his own personal advantage.

Cain changes his profession.

They were competitors in the early days of the railroad business.

The Carpet Seller

The solution can be accomplished in a single cut, but it is not a straight cut.

The two pieces can fit together perfectly to make either a 9 by 16 rectangle or a 12 by 12 square.

The carpet is not used on the stairs, but it may be helpful to think in terms of steps!

Cartoon Character

The scientific journal misstated and exaggerated the properties of something.

The cartoon character was designed to be a sort of role model for children, and to influence their habits.

The cartoon character was intended to make an unpopular but healthy item popular.

Chimney Problem

He came down very slowly.

The chimney was not the same after he finished his descent.

Clean-Shaven

Alexander the Great was interested in military conquest.

He believed that clean-shaven soldiers had an advantage.

Complete Garbage

If the garbage had not been emptied, he would have lived.

He was poor and tired.

He died a violent death.

Dali's Brother

Salvador Dali is recognized as a brilliant surrealist painter.

Salvador Dali's younger brother was actually a brilliant surrealist painter but his older brother never knew this.

The two brothers had something important and unusual in common.

A Day at the Races

The man deserved to be punished.

He had no special influence with the police, and they fully intended to prosecute him.

He had a special skill that he often used to his advantage.

Debugging

Ants were used in the diagnosis of diabetes.

The ants' actions could indicate that a person had diabetes.

Don't Get Up

No one else is in the apartment and she knows that no one else will answer the phone.

She does not know the caller, but she knows that the call is probably important.

She knows the call is not for her.

She has no malicious motives.

88 Too Big

It was a number he chose to use.

He was not at home.

He did not know the right number.

Exceptional Gratitude

Bill thanked Ted for eggs he had never received in order to influence Ted's actions.

They were neighbors.

Ted was lazy and mean.

Fair Fight

The boxer did not expect to collect any money.

The trainer collected a worthwhile sum for his efforts.

The boxer won fairly, but without throwing a punch.

Fill Her Up!

He deliberately ruined the car, but later he deeply regretted his action.

He was a jealous cement truck driver.

Fingerprint Evidence

It was not Bundy's fingerprints or any of his victim's fingerprints that incriminated him, but it was fingerprint evidence.

The police found something unusual when they searched Bundy's apartment.

Fired for Joining Mensa

Anne's employers would not have objected to her joining any other organization.

She was employed in an administrative position, she did her job well, and her employers were pleased with her.

If she had joined Mensa, there may have been a conflict of interest.

Flipping Pages

I did this deliberately in order to produce a specific result.

I could do this only in certain places.

I should have gotten permission from the publisher first.

Free Lunch

The man ate his lunch with one knife and one fork.

He provided a service.

The restaurant provided an intimate atmosphere in the evenings.

Full Refund

It was highly unusual for the theater to give a refund.

The theater manager was glad that they left.

They had acted cruelly.

Garbage Nosiness

I was annoyed with myself, not with my neighbors.

I looked in the cans on the same morning each week.

When I looked in the cans, I saw that they had something in common, which mine did not.

Gas Attack

He did not use the mask to disguise himself or anyone else.

The gas mask was standard issue.

His actions could have saved the lives of many people.

Getting Away with Murder

The man had a longstanding motive to kill her.

He was clearly guilty, but had to be released under the law.

He was punished for this crime.

Golf Bag

Paul removed the bag without touching it.

He did not deliberately set fire to the bag since that would have incurred a penalty.

He indulged in a bad habit.

Happy Birthday

There was nothing about his appearance that indicated it was his birthday.

He was not well known.

She worked in a shop but was not a shop assistant.

She had access to information.

Hosing Down

They used regular water. The road was not contaminated in any way.

It was for a special event.

They did not hose the entire road.

Invisible

It can be made of metal or wood.

It is powerful.

You can see it under some circumstances, but not others, even when it is directly in front of you.

Job Description

She acted on impulse, but she chose them for a specific reason.

The woman was angry because of the men's actions.

She knew they had been talking about her.

Leadfoot and Gumshoe

She and the police officer were strangers and she was not trying to help or impress him.

She was acting from high moral principles, and was also protecting someone's reputation.

Machine Forge

The man sells the machine to a crook.

Although the machine produces perfect $100 bills, it cannot be used to make the crook rich.

Man in Tights

He was knocked out by the rock, but it did not touch him.

He was involved in many dangerous adventures.

He was a well-known sight in his tights.

The Man Who Got Water

He had intended to use the water in connection with his car, but something happened to make him change his mind.

He was very angry.

Missing Items

He grows them.

Everyone has them—men and women.

They are in the lower part of the body.

Misunderstood

Very few, if any, criminals speak this language.

It is chosen for its rarity.

A handful of words are used—but they are important.

Motion Not Passed

Many people voted for the motion, and the poll was performed correctly according to the rules.

If a few more people had voted against the motion, it would have been passed. If many more people had voted against it, then it would have been rejected.

No More Bore

Churchill gave the butler something.

The butler gave the impression that he was misbehaving.

Nonconventional

They are not prohibited from speaking altogether.

The do not use signs, gestures, or codes.

They are extremely courteous and concerned for the well-being of their companions.

Nonexistent Actors

The nonexistent actors had never existed and took no part whatsoever in the movie, but their names were put deliberately into the credits.

It was a murder-mystery movie.

No Response

The question was one that he often answered, and if anyone else had asked it he would have answered.

The content of the question does not matter. It was the way it was asked that matters.

The stranger had a difficulty.

Noteworthy

The criminal had committed a crime in the woman's house.

The criminal had visited the bank.

The picture of the president is well known.

November 11

Although it appeared as though many customers had been born on November 11, the real distribution of births of the company's customers was not unusual.

All the data had been entered on a computer database.

The customers appeared to have birthdays on November 11, 1911.

Once Too Often

You can do this many times in your life.

You do it on a specific day that is not of your choosing.

It is variously considered a right, a privilege, and a duty.

One Mile

The one-mile kink is not associated with any physical or geographical feature of the landscape. The land there is the same as elsewhere along the border.

There was no mistake in the original map and none in the current map.

Actions were taken to speed up the survey of the border.

Pass Protection

Other people could pass through in the same fashion that I did.

As I looked at the people in line, I could see the frustration in their faces.

I always buy a token for every journey.

Pentagon Puzzle

The number of people working there is not relevant.

The reason dates back to when the Pentagon was built.

When it was built, the extra bathrooms were necessary.

Picture Purchase

He was honest and there were no crooked motives involved.

He did not intend to take any action to make the picture more valuable.

He would not have bought the picture if it had been rolled up.

Poor Investment

They could easily buy another of these items; in fact, they had several spare ones.

If it was lost, then it had to be found.

They were looking for information.

The Power of Tourism

The tourists do not consume large amounts of electricity.

The place does not have costly lights or unusual electrical entertainment or appliances.

The place is a famous natural tourist attraction.

Promotion

The company knows exactly what John is like.

Promoting John is part of a clever plan.

They promote him very publicly.

The Ransom Note

The police could glean no clues from the content, paper, or style of the ransom note.

The ransom note was mailed, but the postmark gave no clues.

There were no fingerprints, but the police were able to establish a unique match with the criminal.

Reentry

It is popular.

It is a collection.

Rejected Shoes

The shoes fit him comfortably, but there was something uncomfortable about them.

They were made of different material from his other shoes.

They were fine when worn outside, but not when worn inside.

Replacing the Leaves

The girl is very sad.

She is trying to prevent something from happening.

She is acting on something she heard.

Riddle of the Sphinx

The Sphinx had poetic license. Morning, afternoon, and evening are metaphorical rather than literal times.

Not all the legs are limbs, but they all support the body.

Right Off

He is upset that his new car is ruined, but pleased at something else.

No other vehicle is involved.

He acquires something rare.

Russian Racer

The papers reported accurately, but put the most positive light on the Russian car's performance and the most negative on the American car's.

The papers did not report how many cars raced.

Scuba Do

He had not been diving and had no immediate intention of going diving.

He was an avid diver.

The reason had to do with safety.

Secret Assignment

Knowing the students' habits, he did some clever detective work.

He knew they were serious, studious, and always prepared themselves for assignments.

He checked something in a particular place at the university.

Seven Bells

The shopkeeper could easily change the sign, but chooses not to do so.

No superstition about numbers is involved.

Many people notice the discrepancy.

Shaking a Fist

The man was not a criminal. He had been driving erratically.

There was something unusual about the man.

The policeman quickly knew that the man was in danger.

Shooting a Dead Man

The policeman knew that the man was already dead.

He wanted someone else to see what he was doing.

He was not tampering with evidence. He was trying to get information.

The Shoplifter

She does not stop, because she is in danger of being caught.

She steals under a certain guise that enables her to gradually steal larger items.

She is recognized on her regular circuit, but is not known to be a shoplifter.

Six-Foot Drop

The tomato fell six feet.

It was a regular tomato.

The man was fast.

Slow Drive

There is nothing wrong with the man, the car, the road, or the driving conditions.

This happened under very particular circumstances. At other times he drives at normal speeds.

If he went faster, he would lose something he values.

Spraying the Grass

He wanted the grass to look perfect.

Something was different about the spraying this time.

If he had done this regularly, it would have eventually harmed the grass.

Statue of an Insect

The insect had caused a big problem.

The town's prosperity depends on agriculture.

The insect's actions caused a change.

Straight Ahead

It was not done for economic reasons.

The straight miles make no difference to traffic conditions.

The straight miles were designed for use in extreme circumstances.

Strangulation

She was strangled to death with a scarf.

No dancing was involved.

She should not have been in such a hurry.

Talking to Herself

The man was recording something for his archives.

She held a unique distinction.

The Test

Each boy deserved the grade he was given.

There was something unusual about the test.

Jerry was not as diligent as he should have been.

Three Spirals

It appeared as though she was receiving something for pleasure, but for her it was deadly serious.

She was involved in dangerous and illegal activities.

The spirals contained information.

Two Clocks

They were fully functional clocks that were used to measure time.

The clocks were used only occasionally and never when the man was on his own.

The man had a particular hobby.

The Unbroken Arm

She was not seeking sympathy or help. Nothing was concealed in the cast.

She was about to do something important.

She knew that the plaster cast would be noticed immediately.

Unclimbed

It is not underwater—it is clearly visible aboveground.

It would be very difficult to climb.

Unknown Recognition

The man was physically normal and there was nothing abnormal about his appearance.

I am not related to him, but a relationship is involved.

The Unlucky Bed

All the patients who died were seriously ill, but they were not expected to die.

There is nothing wrong or dangerous about the bed or its location.

No doctors or nurses are involved in the cause of the deaths.

Patients receiving particular treatment are put in this bed.

Up in the Air

It is small.

It does not fly.

Check your assumptions on every word of the puzzle!

Walking Backward

There was no one else in the house.

The man was not afraid of any danger to himself.

He did not know who had rung the bell.

He ran out the back in order to run around to the front of the house.

Waterless Rivers

This is not a physical place.

It has mountains, but you could walk over them easily.

The cities, forests, mountains, and rivers are real places on planet Earth.

Weak Case

He paid his bail fully and promptly, but paying it incriminated him.

He paid in cash, but it was untraceable.

Well-Meaning

There were several of these creatures in a public place.

They were facing death.

She made a false assumption about the conditions necessary for their survival.

Window Pain

Both the windows are perfect squares.

Their areas are different.

They look different.

Winning Numbers

If I participate, I will have the same chance as everyone else.

I am in no way prohibited from playing or winning.

The piece of paper has next week's winning lottery numbers on it. It also has last week's winning numbers.

Wiped Out

She worked as a cleaner in a large building.

She cleaned on every floor.

She did much more work than was necessary.

Wonder Horse

The horse did not deserve to win.

The weather was relevant.

This horse did not work as hard as the other horses in the race.

The Writer

It was a long process.

Somebody helped him.

He used a part of his body that was not paralyzed.

The Wrong Ball

The ball was clearly visible and accessible.

He did not touch the ball or examine it. He knew it wasn't his immediately upon seeing it.

You Can't Be Too Careful

The pure medicine tastes very bitter.

They do not buy it as a medicine, although it is medicine.

It is effective against malaria.

THE ANSWERS

Acidic Action
The woman's body was completely dissolved, but she had a plastic tooth that was not soluble in the acid.

Adolf Hitler
This apparently true incident took place during the first World War when Adolf Hitler was a private in the German army. He was wounded and the British soldier thought it would be unchivalrous to kill him.

Adrift in the Ocean
They are in the vicinity of the mouth of the Amazon River. The outflow of river water is so huge that the Atlantic Ocean in that region consists of fresh water for hundreds of miles.

Alex Ferguson
Alex Ferguson chews gum incessantly during soccer games. The sale and use of chewing gum are illegal in Singapore.

Alone in a Boat
The two animals were skunks that had been ejected from Noah's Ark because of the stench they were causing.

Ancient Antics
No new species of animal has been domesticated in the last 4000 years. The ancients domesticated dogs, cats, cows, sheep, horses, etc.

Angry Response
The man had said he would be home at 8:00 P.M. He arrived the following morning at 8:02 A.M.

Assault and Battery
John is a newborn baby. The doctor slaps him to make him cry and use his lungs.

The Auction
The man was bidding for a parrot that was such a good mimic that it bid against him!

Bald Facts
The woman was French and fell in love with a German officer during the German occupation of France. After the liberation, a mob shaved off all her hair and branded her a collaborator.

Bare Bones
The student was pregnant. She had two femurs of her own, two of her unborn baby, and one in her hands.

Barren Patch
Years earlier a troubled airplane had dumped its fuel onto this patch of land.

Biography
The author wrote the biography of Marie Curie, the great French scientist who made many important discoveries concerning radioactivity. She won two Nobel prizes but died of leukemia caused by radiation. The biographer collected many of her writings, belongings, and experimental apparatuses to help him write about her. Unfortunately, most of the memorabilia were highly contaminated with radioactivity, and he died later as a result of being exposed to it.

Bottled Up
She took home the man's empty champagne bottles after a party. She then left them out with her garbage for collection in order to impress her neighbors.

Burnt Wood
Every two years England plays Australia at cricket for the "Ashes." Its name stems from an epitaph published in

1882 following Australia's first victory over England. The article lamented the death of English cricket and stated that its remains would be cremated. The following year the ashes of a burnt cricket stump were presented in an urn to the captain of the English team. The urn has remained ever since at Lord's Cricket Club in London. Each "Ashes" series consists of five or six five-day matches that are fiercely contested and generate a huge following in both countries.

Business Rivalry
Cain and Abel were rival train operators involved in the shipping of cattle by rail. When Abel lowered his shipping rates well below cost, Cain dropped out of the rail business and instead bought all the cattle he could find, making a fortune by shipping them to market on Abel's trains.

The Carpet Seller
The cut is made, in feet, as shown below.

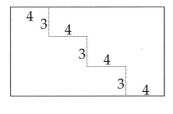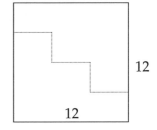

Cartoon Character
The cartoon character who owes his existence to a misprint in a scientific journal is Popeye. He was invented to encourage children to eat spinach, which was thought to contain large amounts of iron. But this information was based on an error in a scientific journal—the decimal point had been put in the wrong place, making the iron content of spinach appear ten times higher than it actually was.

Chimney Problem
The man on the tall chimney had a penknife in his pocket. With this he pried loose a brick from the top layer. He used the brick as a hammer. In this way, he gradually demolished the chimney by knocking out all the bricks and lowered himself to the ground.

Clean-Shaven
Bearded men could be grabbed by the beard in close combat.

Complete Garbage
The man was sleeping in a garbage can that was taken to the compactor.

Dali's Brother
Salvador Dali died at age 7. Nine months later his brother was born and was also named Salvador. It was the younger Salvador Dali who became the famous surrealist painter.

A Day at the Races
The man was a thief who had made money at the races by picking pockets. After the policeman took down all his details, the man picked the policeman's pocket. The policeman returned to the station with no written record. He didn't remember the details because he didn't think he would need to remember them.

Debugging
If ants gathered around the place where a person had urinated, it was a strong indication that the person had diabetes. The ants were attracted by the sugar in the urine.

Don't Get Up
The woman lives in an apartment building. She hears the phone ringing in the adjacent apartment. She knows that her neighbor, who is a brain surgeon, is out.

88 Too Big

The man was an English tourist in the U.S. He was alone in an apartment when he had a heart attack. He crawled to the phone and dialed the English emergency number, 999, instead of the 911 used in America.

Exceptional Gratitude

Bill and Ted were neighbors. Ted kept chickens. Ted's chickens had been wandering through a gap in his fence and pecking around in Bill's garden. They had never laid an egg there. But after Bill thanked Ted for the eggs that his chickens had laid, Ted quickly fixed the fence to stop the chickens from getting out.

Fair Fight

The boxer was a dog that had just won the championship at a dog show.

Fill Her Up!

The woman saved carefully and bought her husband the car as a surprise anniversary present. She had it delivered into their driveway and completed the paperwork with the salesman who brought it. Her husband was a cement truck driver. He was jealous and suspicious. He came home unexpectedly, and when he saw the new car in his driveway and his wife talking to a smartly dressed stranger, he assumed the worst. He reversed his truck and dumped his truck's load into the car.

Fingerprint Evidence
When Bundy's apartment was searched, none of his fingerprints were found. This fact was used by the prosecution as evidence of his compulsion to clean fingerprints in all situations—showing his guilt.

Fired for Joining Mensa
Anne works for Mensa in the administration of admission tests. Under Mensa's constitution, no member can be an employee.

Flipping Pages
I was photocopying the book.

Free Lunch
The man was a piano tuner who had come to tune the piano in the restaurant. He brought his own tuning fork. The restaurateur repaid the service with a free lunch.

Full Refund
The couple had a little baby with them. They were allowed into the theater on the condition that they leave if the baby cried, with their money refunded. After about 20 minutes, they realized that the movie was terrible, so the mother pinched her baby to make it cry. They left with a refund.

Garbage Nosiness
On our street we put the cans out on the curb for collection every Monday morning. I forgot to put the can out two weeks in a row. Looking in my neighbor's can was the easiest way to confirm that I had missed the collection.

Gas Attack

The unfortunate man was August Jager who had served in the German army in World War I. He was sentenced to ten years' imprisonment in 1932 for treason. He had deserted in 1915 and been taken by the French just before the Germans launched the first-ever poison gas attack. The French asked him what his gas mask was and he told them. Ironically, it was only in 1930, when the French General Ferry wrote his memoirs, that it was revealed that Jager had told the French about the impending attack. The French ignored the information and took no evasive action. However, the German court found Jager guilty of treason in view of the fact that he had not thrown away his gas mask.

Getting Away with Murder

Many years earlier, the man's wife had faked her own murder and had run off with her lover. The man had been tried for her murder and convicted. He had served a 20-year sentence. When released, he found her and shot her, but he could not be convicted of the same crime twice.

Golf Bag

To deliberately ignite the paper bag would be to interfere with his lie and incur a penalty. So while he pondered the problem he smoked a cigarette. He discarded the cigarette onto the bag and it burned. No penalty was incurred.

Happy Birthday

The man went to the eye doctor to have an eye test. The doctor looked at his record and noticed that today was his birthday.

Hosing Down

This incident occurred just before the start of the Monaco Grand Prix race, which is held in the streets of Monte

Carlo. Part of the course runs through a tunnel. When it rains outside, the firemen hose down the road in the tunnel in order to make the surface wet. This improves consistency and safety.

Invisible
The object is an airplane propeller, which rotates so fast that it cannot be seen.

Job Description
The two men were sitting by the window in the restaurant. As the woman passed, one of the men made sexist remarks to the other man, implying that the woman made her living by immoral means. She stormed into the restaurant and went up to them and said, "Actually, I am a lipreader."

Leadfoot and Gumshoe
The woman is the wife of the chief of police. In order to avoid any impression of favoritism she accepted the ticket and paid the fine.

Machine Forge
This true story concerns a confidence trickster. He sells the machine to a crook claiming it will generate perfect forgeries. He demonstrates the machine by feeding in green paper. But this green paper is actually genuine $100 bills covered in thick green coloring. The machine simply removes the green coloring.

Man in Tights
The man was Superman. He was lying next to a block of kryptonite, the one thing that could knock him out.

The Man Who Got Water
This is a true story from Russia. The man had intended to wash his car, but when he returned he found that it had been stolen.

Missing Items
The 10-year-old boy has kneecaps, which babies do not have. These develop between the ages of 2 and 5.

Misunderstood
The instructions given to police dogs are normally in a language not often spoken in the U.S., such as Hungarian or Czech. This is to make it unlikely that any person other than the trained police officers will be able to control the dog.

Motion Not Passed
Although 35% of the people voted for the referendum motion and 14% against, there were not enough votes overall for a quorum to be reached. It needed 50% of the population to vote in order for the results to be valid. If another 1% had voted against the motion, it would have carried.

No More Bore
Winston Churchill told his butler to go to the door smoking one of Churchill's finest cigars.

Nonconventional
If a nun wants the salt, she asks the nun nearest the salt if she would like the mustard, which is near the first nun. The second nun would reply, "No, but do you want the salt?"

Nonexistent Actors
The movie is *Sleuth*, starring Laurence Olivier and Michael Caine only. If moviegoers were not fooled into thinking that there were other actors involved, it would give the plot away. At one stage Caine leaves and returns in disguise.

No Response
The man had a stutter. The stranger who asked him the question also had a stutter. The man thought that if he answered and stuttered, then the stranger would think that he was being mocked, so the man decided not to answer.

Noteworthy
A burglar had broken into the woman's house and taken all her savings. In trying to collect the last bill that was stuffed into a jar, he tore it in half. She reported the incident to the police, and then took the half of the bill to her bank. They told her that a man had been in that morning with the matching half!

November 11
When data entry clerks entered customer records onto the computer, the date field had to be completed. However, they often did not have that data, so they simply keyed in 11/11/11.

Once Too Often
Voting twice in the same election is electoral fraud—a serious offense.

One Mile
When it was originally surveyed, two teams were sent out down the west side of South Dakota. One started from the north and one from the south. They missed! It was easier to put the kink in the border than to redo the survey.

Pass Protection
I am describing the end of my journey. My destination is a subway station that is a starting point for many commuters. I bought and used a token at the start of my trip. I simply exit through the turnstiles, passing the lines of commuters coming in.

Pentagon Puzzle
The Pentagon was built in the 1940s, when the state of Virginia had strict segregation laws requiring that blacks and whites use different bathrooms.

Picture Purchase
The picture was worthless, but it was in a fine frame that he intended to reuse.

Poor Investment
The object is the black box flight recorder from a crashed jetliner.

The Power of Tourism
The place is Niagara Falls, where the water can be diverted from the falls in order to power generators. If the beautiful view of the waterfall were not demanded by the tourists, then much of the water could be channeled through turbines to provide electricity, thus lowering the price.

Promotion
John was promoted very publicly. He was immediately headhunted by a rival firm, and lured away with a salary he could not resist. The original company wanted to fire him, but that would have been costly. They knew that their rivals were desperate to recruit one of their top people. This way, they got rid of him and saddled their rivals with a dud.

The Ransom Note
The police were able to get a DNA trace from the saliva on the back of the stamp. This matched the suspect's DNA.

Reentry
The Guinness Book of Records, after 19 years of publication, became the second-best-selling book of all time and therefore got into itself.

Rejected Shoes
The man found that the synthetic shoes generated a buildup of static electricity when he wore them around his carpeted office. He constantly got electric shocks, so he rejected them and went back to his old leather shoes.

Replacing the Leaves
The girl has a fatal disease. She overheard the doctor tell her mother that by the time all the leaves have fallen from the trees she will be dead.

Riddle of the Sphinx
The answer is man, who crawls on all fours as a child, walks on two legs as an adult, and uses a walking stick in old age.

Right Off
In this true incident, the car had been struck and destroyed by a large meteorite that the man found lying next to the car. The meteorite was rare and it was bought by a museum for over one million dollars.

Russian Racer
The Russian newspaper reported (correctly) that the American car came in next to last while the Russian car came in second.

Scuba Do
The man, who was nearsighted, was on a diving vacation. He had broken his glasses and wore the diving mask, which had prescription lenses, in order to see properly.

Secret Assignment
Ulam went to the university library and examined the library records of all the books borrowed by his students over the previous month. Los Alamos was a common link to nearly all of them.

Seven Bells
It was originally a mistake, but the shopkeeper found that so many people came into his shop to point out the error that it increased his business.

Shaking a Fist
The man suffered from severe allergic reactions to certain foods. He had inadvertently eaten something that had caused him to have a fit while driving. He veered across the road and came to a stop. He was unable to speak, but waved his hand at the policeman. He was wearing a bracelet indicating his condition. The policeman was therefore able to call for appropriate medical help.

Shooting a Dead Man
This puzzle is based on an incident in the film *The Untouchables*. There had been a shootout at a house and the police had captured a gangster who was refusing to give them the information they wanted. Sean Connery went outside and propped up against the window the body of another gangster, who had died earlier. Pretending the man was alive, he threatened him and then shot him. The prisoner was then convinced that Connery would stop at nothing to get the information he wanted. The prisoner talked.

The Shoplifter
The shoplifter is a woman who pretends to be pregnant. She has a whole range of false "bellies" under her coat. After nine months, she naturally has to stop.

Six-Foot Drop
He caught it just above the ground.

Slow Drive
The man was moving. He was a beekeeper. In his car he had a queen bee. His swarm of bees was flying with the car to follow the queen bee.

Spraying the Grass
This happened just prior to the 1996 Atlanta Olympics. The groundskeeper sprayed the grass with organic green paint in order to make it look greener for the television audiences.

Statue of an Insect
The insect is the boll weevil, which wreaked havoc with the local cotton crop. As a result, many of the farmers switched to growing peanuts—and became very rich when peanut prices rose.

Straight Ahead
The straight sections were specified so that they could be used as aircraft landing strips in case of war or emergency.

Strangulation
The famous dancer was Isadora Duncan, who was strangled when the long scarf she was wearing caught in the wheel of her sports car.

Talking to Herself
The woman was 87. The language she was speaking was dying out and she was the last person to know it. The man was an academic who filmed her to record the language before it was lost forever. (This puzzle is based on the true story of Dr. David Dalby's filming the last woman to speak the African language of Bikya.)

The Test
The final instruction in the test was to ignore all the previous questions. The teacher had repeatedly told the students to read over the entire exam before beginning. The test was given to see how well the pupils could follow instructions.

Three Spirals
The woman was a spy. She received record albums in the mail. When they were intercepted, they were found to contain music. However, one side had two separate spirals, one inside the other. The inner groove contained the secret information. She was caught when the authorities noticed that one side of the record lasted only half as long as the other.

Two Clocks
The man was an avid chess player. His wife gave him a chess clock. This consists of two identical clocks in one housing. Each clock records the time taken by one player for his moves in a competitive chess game.

The Unbroken Arm
The healthy young girl put a cast on her arm before going to take a French oral examination. She figured (correctly) that the examiner would ask her about her injury. She came to the exam prepared with answers about how she broke it.

Unclimbed
The largest-known extinct volcano is Mons Olympus on Mars.

Unknown Recognition
He was the identical twin brother of someone I knew well. I had heard of him but had never met him before.

The Unlucky Bed
Every Friday morning, a cleaning woman comes to the ward with a vacuum cleaner. The most convenient electrical socket is the one to which the patient's life support machine is connected. She unplugs this for a few minutes while she does her work. The noise of the vacuum cleaner covers the patient's dying gasps. The cleaner reconnects the machine and goes to the next ward. (Although this story was reported as factual in a South African newspaper, it is almost certainly an urban legend.)

Up in the Air
A dead centipede!

Walking Backward
The man walked backward from the front door as he varnished the wooden floor. He left the front door open for

ventilation. When someone rang the doorbell, he quickly ran around to the front of the house in order to stop the person from walking inside onto the wet varnish.

Waterless Rivers
A map.

Weak Case
The police charged the man with stealing coins from a vending machine. He was given bail of $400, which he paid for entirely in quarters.

Well-Meaning
The animal rights activist went into a restaurant where there were live lobsters in a tank. She bought them all to liberate them, but freed them into fresh water, where they all died because they can live only in salt water.

Window Pain
Initially the square window has sides of about 1.4 feet and an area of 2 square feet. It is as shown below. The second window has sides of 2 feet and an area of 4 square feet.

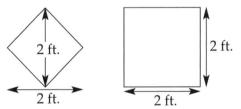

Winning Numbers
One has to choose six numbers from 60 for the lotto jackpot. My piece of paper contains all 60 numbers, so it must contain the winning numbers.

Wiped Out
The woman had been told to clean the elevators in a skyscraper. She had cleaned the same elevator on each floor!

Wonder Horse
In this true story, the race consisted of three laps. It was a very misty day. One of the horses stopped at the far side, of course, waited a lap for the other horses to come around, then rejoined the race and won. The jockey later confessed.

The Writer
He winked one eye and thereby indicated to a very dedicated assistant each letter, word, and sentence of the book. He was Jean-Dominique Bauby, the French writer. The book he wrote by blinking, *The Diving Bell and the Butterfly*, was published just before his death in 1996 and became a bestseller.

The Wrong Ball
It had been a cold night and the ball was lying in a small frozen puddle.

You Can't Be Too Careful
The medicine is quinine, which is used to treat malaria and which people buy in tonic water. The British in India suffered badly from malaria until it was discovered that quinine cured and prevented it. Quinine tasted unpleasant, so they put it into carbonated water and created tonic water.

WALLY Test I Answers

Here are the answers to the first WALLY Test. Be prepared to groan!

1. Your feet off the floor.
2. A ditch.
3. Albert. (He deferred to Queen Victoria's wish that no future king be called Albert.)
4. A walk!
5. There are 204 squares of varying sizes on a regular eight-by-eight chessboard.
6. 12—the second of January, the second of February, etc.
7. He throws it straight up.
8. Greenland. Australia is a continental landmass.
9. He does not have a door in his pajamas.
10. 5 minutes.

Rate your score on the following scale:

Number Correct	Rating
8 to 10	WALLY Whiz
6 to 7	Smart Aleck
3 to 5	WALLY
0 to 2	Ultra-WALLY

WALLY Test II Answers

More answers, more groans!

1. ONE NEW WORD.
2. The letter N.
3. Neither—"Seven eights are 56."
4. They threw one cigarette away, thus making the boat a cigarette lighter.
5. 11 seconds. There are 11 intervals as opposed to 5.
6. Whoever the current U.S. president is. His name then was the same as it is today.
7. Tom Hanks and Carl Lewis.
8. No time—you can't have half a hole.
9. He broke out with measles!
10. You should stick in on the package, not on yourself!

Rate your score on the following scale:

Number Correct	Rating
8 to 10	WALLY Whiz
6 to 7	Smart Aleck
3 to 5	WALLY
0 to 2	Ultra-WALLY

About the Authors

PAUL SLOANE was born in Scotland and educated at Cambridge University, where he studied engineering. He has worked for many years in the computer industry, primarily in international software marketing. He has always been an avid collector and creator of lateral thinking puzzles. His first book, *Lateral Thinking Puzzlers*, was published by Sterling in 1991, and has gone on to become a bestseller. It has been translated into many languages. Following its success, he established himself as the leading expert in this kind of conundrum. He runs the lateral thinking puzzle forum on the Web at www.books.com and has his own home page. He is an acclaimed speaker on lateral thinking in business. He lives with his wife in Camberley, England. He has three daughters, and tries to keep fit by playing chess, tennis, and golf.

DES MACHALE was born in County Mayo, Ireland, and is Associate Professor of Mathematics at University College in Cork. He and his wife, Anne, have five children.

The author of over 40 books, including one on the John Ford cult film *The Quiet Man* and another on George Boole of Boolean algebra fame, Des MacHale has many interests. He has a large collection of crystals, minerals, rocks, and fossils; he was chairman of the International Conference on Humor in 1985; and his hobbies include broadcasting, film, photography, and numismatics. In fact, he is interested in just about everything except wine, jazz, and Demi Moore.

This is the sixth book coauthored by Paul Sloane and Des MacHale, following the success of their other lateral thinking puzzle books, also published by Sterling.

Index

Acidic Action, 21, *50*, **74**

Adolf Hitler, 16, *50*, **74**

Adrift in the Ocean, 34, *50*, **74**

Alex Ferguson, 23, *50*, **74**

Alone in a Boat, 10, *50*, **74**

Ancient Antics, 44, *51*, **74**

Angry Response, 10, *51*, **74**

Assault and Battery, 15, *51*, **74**

Auction, The, 32, *52*, **75**

Bald Facts, 39, *52*, **75**

Bare Bones, 29, *52*, **75**

Barren Patch, 34, *52*, **75**

Biography, 44, *52*, **75**

Bottled Up, 23, *53*, **75**

Burnt Wood, 36, *53*, **75–76**

Business Rivalry, 47, *53*, **76**

Carpet Seller, 45, *53*, **76**

Cartoon Character, 45, *54*, **76**

Chimney Problem, 20, *54*, **77**

Clean-Shaven, 16, *54*, **77**

Complete Garbage, 11, *54*, **77**

Dali's Brother, 29, *54*, **77**

Day at the Races, A, 48, *55*, **77**

Debugging, 43, *55*, **77**

Don't Get Up, 23, *55*, **77**

88 Too Big, 31, *55*, **78**

Exceptional Gratitude, 28, *55*, **78**

Fair Fight, 16, *56*, **78**

Fill Her Up!, 41, *56*, **78–79**

Fingerprint Evidence, 39, *56*, **79**

Fired for Joining Mensa, 14, *56*, **79**

Flipping Pages, 12, *56*, **79**

Free Lunch, 47, *57*, **79**

Full Refund, 47, *57*, **79**

Garbage Nosiness, 21, *57*, **79**

Gas Attack, 37, *57*, **80**

Getting Away with Murder, 28, *57*, **80**

Golf Bag, 11, *58*, **80**

Happy Birthday, 21, *58*, **80**

Hosing Down, 40, *58*, **80–81**

Invisible, 31, *58*, **81**

Job Description, 34, *58–59*, **81**

Leadfoot and Gumshoe, 12, *59*, **81**

Machine Forge, 33, *59*, **81**

Man in Tights, 12, *59*, **81**

Man Who Got Water, The, 20, *59*, **81**

Missing Items, 18, *59*, **82**

Misunderstood, 23, *60*, **82**

Motion Not Passed, 13, *60*, **82**

No More Bore, 35, *60*, **82**
Nonconventional, 41, *60*, **82**
Nonexistent Actors, 33, *60*, **82**
No Response, 46, *61*, **82**
Noteworthy, 18, *61*, **83**
November 11, 21, *61*, **83**

Once Too Often, 18, *61*, **83**
One Mile, 26, *61–62*, **83**

Pass Protection, 48, *62*, **83**
Pentagon Puzzle, 40, *62–63*, **83**
Picture Purchase, 10, *63*, **84**
Poor Investment, 32, *63*, **84**
Power of Tourism, The, 30, *63*, **84**
Promotion, 34, *63*, **84**

Ransom Note, The, 43, *64*, **84**
Reentry, 15, *64*, **84**
Rejected Shoes, 19, *64*, **84**
Replacing the Leaves, 42, *64*, **85**
Riddle of the Sphinx, 17, *64*, **85**
Right Off, 47, *65*, **85**
Russian Racer, 13, *65*, **85**

Scuba Do, 24, *65*, **85**
Secret Assignment, 42, *65*, **85**
Seven Bells, 15, *65–66*, **85**
Shaking a Fist, 35, *66*, **86**
Shooting a Dead Man, 22, *66*, **86**
Shoplifter, The, 27, *66*, **86**
Six-Foot Drop, 15, *66*, **86**
Slow Drive, 19, *67*, **86**

Spraying the Grass, 33, *67*, **86**
Statue of an Insect, 14, *67*, **87**
Straight Ahead, 12, *67*, **87**
Strangulation, 10, *67*, **87**

Talking to Herself, 17, *68*, **87**
Test, The, 13, *68*, **87**
Three Spirals, 41, *68*, **87**
Two Clocks, 30, *68*, **88**

Unbroken Arm, The, 27, *68*, **88**
Unclimbed, 17, *69*, **88**
Unknown Recognition, 16–17, *69*, **88**
Unlucky Bed, The, 18, *69*, **88**
Up in the Air, 15, *69*, **88**

Walking Backward, 46, *69*, **88–89**
WALLY Test I, 25, **91**
WALLY Test II, 38, **92**
Waterless Rivers, 13, *70*, **89**
Weak Case, 20, *70*, **89**
Well-Meaning, 22, *70*, **89**
Window Pain, 37, *70*, **89**
Winning Numbers, 16, *70*, **89**
Wiped Out, 31, *71*, **89**
Wonder Horse, 33, *71*, **90**
Writer, The, 20, *71*, **90**
Wrong Ball, The, 36, *71*, **90**

You Can't Be Too Careful, 41, *71*, **90**

Page key:
puzzle, *clues*, **answer**

Lateral Thinking Puzzle Books
by Paul Sloane and Des MacHale

••

Lateral Thinking Puzzlers
Paul Sloane, 1991
0-8069-8227-6

Challenging Lateral Thinking Puzzles
Paul Sloane & Des MacHale, 1993
0-8069-8671-9

Great Lateral Thinking Puzzles
Paul Sloane & Des MacHale, 1994
0-8069-0553-0

Test Your Lateral Thinking IQ
Paul Sloane, 1994
0-8069-0684-7

Improve Your Lateral Thinking: Puzzles to Challenge Your Mind
Paul Sloane & Des MacHale, 1995
0-8069-1374-6

Intriguing Lateral Thinking Puzzles
Paul Sloane & Des MacHale, 1996
0-8069-4252-5

Perplexing Lateral Thinking Puzzles
Paul Sloane & Des MacHale, 1997
0-8069-9769-2

Ingenious Lateral Thinking Puzzles
Paul Sloane & Des MacHale, 1998
0-8069-6259-3

••

Ask for them wherever books are sold.